Ask Me Lord, I Want to Say Yes

Ask Me Lord, I Want to Say Yes

Rosalind Rinker

Logos International
Plainfield, New Jersey

Scripture is taken from the King James
Version (KJV), Revised Standard Version
(RSV), and Today's English Version (TEV),
as indicated.

Ask Me, Lord, I Want to Say Yes
Copyright © 1979 by Rosalind Rinker
All rights reserved
Library of Congress Catalog Card Number: 79-53030
International Standard Book Number: 0-88270-381-1
Logos International, Plainfield, New Jersey 07060
PRINTED IN THE UNITED STATES OF AMERICA

Table of Contents

PART I: My Personal Testimony

Early Recollections.............................3

Three Meditations 7

1 Release from Prejudice 13

2 Learning from the Lutherans
  and the Episcopalians 21

3 The Baptism of the Spirit 31

4 God's Gifts Cannot Be Programmed 37

5 A Methodist Conference in Florida 43

6 God's Gift Given in Praise 51

7 A New Church Home 57

PART II: The Gift of a Prayer Language

8 How Important Is This Gift? 65

9 What Is the Purpose of This Gift? 69

10 What Purpose Does the Prayer
   Language Have in Our Personal Lives? 77

11 What Is the Valid Sign of Having
   Received the Baptism of the Spirit? 85

12 My Friends Share Their Testimonies 95

Recommended Reading 105

Ask Me Lord, I Want to Say Yes

PART I:

My Personal Testimony

Early Recollections

Accepting Jesus Christ as my personal Savior when I was fifteen years old changed my entire life. Immediately I volunteered for missionary service, and as soon as high school was finished, I entered a Bible school. From there I went to China as a missionary-secretary when I was twenty years old, and served there with The Oriental Missionary Society for fourteen years.

Because of political unrest, I was unable to return to China, and completed college at Asbury College in Wilmore, Kentucky. At once I applied and was accepted as a staff member for Inter-Varsity Christian Fellowship, where I served for another fourteen years.

At the close of that time, I became a freelance

writer and speaker, and in the intervening years have traveled thousands of miles in Europe, South America, Canada, and the United States—with a trip to Australia coming up directly. This is my thirteenth book, and two of them have been bestsellers.

Through all these years, my love and loyalty have been centered on Jesus Christ, my Lord, rather than on theology or organization; I have "worked through" the programming given to me in early youth through various paradoxical teachings. I am grateful for the leading of the Holy Spirit, who has been my guide, and for all the experiences He has sent my way.

My early experiences with the Holy Spirit and consequent struggles with the "second blessing" of sanctification are told in my autobiography, *Within the Circle*, and the study guide for that book, especially in chapter four.

The experiences related in this book follow that fourteen-year period with IVCF, when I let the whole subject (the fullness of the Spirit) lie dormant, as it were, while I gave myself to the study of the atonement, the deity of our Lord, prayer, and Bible study. These I taught to students I ministered to in the Pacific Northwest, in the New York City area, in California. Later this material became the foundation for the books and speaking of the past twenty years.

4

Each one of us travels the road of life as though it were laid out for us, but we are profoundly influenced by those whose opinions we value, by the books we read, and by the choices we make.

Increasingly, the message given to me is this: God loves you unconditionally; Jesus Christ came to give you a new life, and to assist you in dealing with the obstacles of that new life. My hope is that you will yield and respond to that love, with open hands and an open heart, in order to receive all the love He has to give you.

I am the good Shepherd.
My sheep hear my voice and they follow Me.
I know my sheep and they know me.
I call them by name and lead them out.[1]

Three Meditations

This cry from my heart is real and honest.
I mean every word, and I repeat it over and over.
   I want to say "Yes" to my Lord's voice.
   I delight to say "Yes" when He speaks to me.
Deep within me, I lay down my own will,
   my own plans,
   yes, even my prejudices
   and my rights.
I lay them, with my self, at His feet:
   Lord, I am Yours.
   I am Your willing child.
   I am Your willing servant.
   Ask me. Speak to me.
   Direct me. Lead me.
   Your love has totally won my heart.

I trust You to prepare me for whatever You send to me.
I trust Your unchangeable love
Even when I cannot understand.

2

There is nothing wrong with my hearing: I can hear all right, but I can't always listen.

Listening has been one of my problems ever since I was a little girl. My alibi is that my mind is so quick! It jumps from one related thing to another, and so I lose track of what is being said.

This is inexcusable sin number one. For when I do not listen to my brother, I sin against love.

How can I love another if I do not listen?

I know. If I listen I will love more and will understand more, both for myself and for the one who is speaking.

Even to this day, although I've worked hard on this problem, my sister will say, "Ros, you aren't listening to me."

Or in a conversation, I'll suddenly say, "What were you talking about?" And the family will laugh and say, "There she goes again . . . not listening. Where were you, Ros?" And I laugh and say, "I'm sorry." And I really am.

Discipline in focusing my attention on the person who is speaking is a lesson in concentration.

I know I'm doing better, because someone told me I was! I've learned to sit quietly and care about you while you are speaking to me, and to look you right in your eyes. That is the best secret I have to share. Love the person who is talking to you.

The result will be: You hear not only what is being said, but what is not being said.

That is love.

Love is listening.

3

My heart cries out:

Lord, forgive me for the times You have spoken to me and I have not listened.

Forgive me for the times You have spoken to me, and I have been too busy to get the message.

Forgive me for the times I have argued with myself, about what I thought I heard You say, and finally sided with my own opinion.

Thank You for not giving up on me.

Thank You for coming back again and again, until I was ready to hear, and open to listening and to obedience.

Forgive me for leaving the word *obedience* out of my vocabulary for so long. I even left it out of some of my books—for I am not a fully obedient child—yet You have released Your unconditional love for me.

My Lord answers:
My child, let me help you build on those negative things, and redeem them all.
I love you unconditionally.
My love is not based on your performance.
There isn't one thing you can do to make Me love you more.
Nor is there one thing you can do to make Me love you less.
I love you, because
I AM LOVE.

My reply:
Tell me over and over, for I forget so soon. I am aware of Your great love for me, and I have centered on that subject, because it is also my greatest need. I have written of Your love, and taught others. The miracle is, that they believe it!
I worship You in quiet thanksgiving.
Thank You, Lord Jesus, for loving me.
Thank You for accepting me.
Thank You for caring about me.
Thank You for the forgiveness of all my sins.
I love You, and I belong to You.

Chapter One

Release from Prejudice

Release from prejudice (programmed ideas) is a painful experience, and the cost is usually reckoned in tears, confusion, pain, and temporary disorientation—until freedom, beautiful freedom, comes.

Several years ago I was one of a number of speakers invited for a Lenten program at a certain pentecostal church. After one of my talks, I was invited to the home of one of the members for lunch.

"Have you received the baptism of the Spirit?" asked my hostess.

"Yes, thanks be to God."

"Had you received the baptism when you wrote those books on the table? Did you speak in tongues?"

When I told her I had not, she replied, "Well, don't you think you should burn all those books you wrote, and start over again, *after* you have received the gift of tongues?"

You can imagine my amazement! Her remarks only served to add more fuel to the early adolescent prejudices I already had concerning the baptism of the Spirit and speaking in tongues. Our church called it by a slightly different name, the filling of the Spirit—and speaking in tongues was an unmentionable (almost heretical) subject.

This incident took place when I was well into my third career—writing and speaking. I have experienced the presence of Christ, my risen Lord, all through my various ministries, as well as the power of the Holy Spirit enabling me to love and to serve Him and to feed His sheep.

My first career began when I was only twenty years old, in mainland China where I lived for fourteen years, serving under The Oriental Missionary Society: first as a secretary and later as a teacher and evangelist in rural areas. During this time I thought only certain churches had the "truth" regarding salvation and the Holy Spirit, and all others were missing out on God's best plan.

Prejudice was planted within me at an early age, and I found it very difficult to recognize, let alone dislodge.

My second career came when China's doors

closed, and I returned to the States and finished my college work at Asbury College in Kentucky. Then for fourteen years I was a staff counselor with Inter-Varsity Christian Fellowship in the Pacific Northwest and New York City. I am continually meeting my former students, who are now in responsible positions and professions, and who remind me of the wonderful ways God worked in our midst at that time.

During the years mentioned above, I'll admit to laying aside the whole subject of the Holy Spirit, including any personal experience with Him. It was during this time I made a thorough study of the Person and Work of our Lord, and wrote the book, *Who Is This Man?*, which helped students discover for themselves (through the study of Mark) the importance of the deity of our Lord. These stabilizing truths were needed to assure them of the security of their sonship in the family of God, for personal faith is based on the fact of Christ's Person and His death and resurrection—not on our feelings.

When I left IVCF, my third career began at the age of fifty with the writing of one of my bestsellers, *Prayer—Conversing with God.* [1] Twenty years have gone by, with thirteen books on record, and thousands of miles by air to hundreds of churches of all denominations. The Lord has given me a ministry of conducting workshops, teaching prayer and

[1] Rinker, Rosalind (Grand Rapids, Michigan: Zondervan, 1959).

personal evangelism all over the United States, Canada, South America, Europe, Japan, Taiwan and Bermuda.

None of this could ever have been accomplished without the indwelling power of the Holy Spirit—who guided me, taught me, empowered me and gave me gifts to build up the body of Christ.

The incident I told at the beginning of this chapter took place about ten years ago, and many others followed quickly. The Lord in His faithfulness was bringing me face to face with more of His truth and showing me how it all fits together. He was also preparing me to face judgmental sins, in order that I might be sent to any of His people, no matter what they taught or believed.

Actually, two of my books do relate personal experiences through which many prejudices were laid aside: *Communicating Love Through Prayer*, and *Within the Circle*.

Then another incident was told to me: A well-known pastor and radio personality forbade his people to read any of my books, because, he said, "She's pentecostal." He continued to hold this idea, in spite of the fact that a close friend of mine was a member of his congregation and told him that he was misinformed. I was deeply offended, because there was no truth in it.

What was true, however, was that all of us were blindly prejudiced in different directions.

The church woman was prejudiced by her denomination to believe that unless one received the gift of tongues, he did not possess the baptism of the Spirit.

The pastor just mentioned was prejudiced; seeing the work of the Holy Spirit in my life, he automatically labeled me "pentecostal" and, therefore, fanatical.

I, too, was prejudiced! I believed I had received the Holy Spirit and through ministry had experienced His power, but I was unwilling to be identified with those who did not hold to our particular interpretation. I simply kept quiet about it, and gave my attention to teaching other subjects.

However, now that healing has come, and I am "one of them," I can see that it is the same Holy Spirit I yielded to as a teenager who is with me now.

I was more "charismatic" than I knew!

How to Cope with Prejudice

How does a child of God recognize and cope with prejudice? The answer is contained in the question.

A child of God will be open to the leading of the Spirit, and when he is willing to look at the many things God puts in his pathway to show him, the truth will finally dawn on him.

In some circles, prejudice is so strong that the very mention of *the baptism* makes the word *tongues* a bad word. This peculiar and precious gift of tongues, used without knowledge and love, can become a tool to separate members of the body of Christ, sow discord among the brethren, and prevent brothers and sisters from loving one another.

And should I, a servant of Christ and a child of God, despise or reject any of the gifts of the Spirit, or any of God's children, because I cannot agree on the name of the pigeonhole by which to file one's religious experience?

Why is there such a strong feeling against the baptism of the Holy Spirit when the Scriptures plainly state (Luke 3:16) that Jesus himself is the baptizer? Did you ever notice that the letters of the apostle Paul are all written to Spirit-baptized believers? To be baptized in the Spirit was the "norm" for believers in the early church.

The Reverend Alfred Durrance of Ocala, Florida, in whose church I have spoken, stated, "Tongues is not the problem; getting it out of perspective is the problem."

Here is a list of things I've come up with that could color our thinking and account for our prejudices:

1. The liturgical churches teach and practice that a person receives the Holy Spirit at water baptism. The evangelicals believe that every born-again person is indwelt by the Holy Spirit. So . . . why

should anyone ask again?

2. Tongues-speaking is not intellectually understood, and for many this is an insurmountable barrier.

3. Others will tell you that their church tradition and theology does not include such phenomena.

4. The actions of unwise and untaught possessors of this baptism turn people off.

5. Finally, the gift of tongues is an affront to the pride of man. Why humble oneself to be willing to pray in a language not understood?

In spite of these objections, you have to admit that wherever there is a counterfeit object, the genuine does exist.

Personally, I have not been able to avoid seeing that unbelievable love does exist between brothers and sisters of the Roman Catholic church and the Lutheran church who have been baptized by the Holy Spirit.

The fruit of the Spirit, which is love, has an unmistakable aroma! (2 Corinthians 2:14-15, Galatians 5:22-23)

A childlike exercise:
In that list of things that account for prejudice, if you saw yourself in any one of them, become

like a little child and ask Jesus to open your mind and to give you a willing heart to let Him heal you of that prejudice. (See Acts 9:9-22, illustrating healing of prejudice.)

Chapter Two

Learning from the Lutherans and the Episcopalians

My first clear understanding about the baptism of the Holy Spirit and the gifts of the Spirit came through contact with the Lutheran church, and later through the Episcopal church.

The first charismatic conference of the Lutheran church was held in Minneapolis in 1971. My friend Lorrie Carlson, who has a Lutheran background, and I were living in Chicago at the time, and decided that we would like to know what was going on.

Pastor Mjorud, chairman of the conference, was very careful at the opening of each service to explain to visiting Lutheran pastors (and there were dozens of new ones at each service) just what was meant by the gift of tongues, which continues to be a big barrier for many people.

The Gift of Tongues Explained

His explanations helped me, too. This is not a direct quotation, but it is what I remember:

There are two gifts of an unknown tongue. The first is for the devotional life of the believer, to aid in the maturing process. The second is for the edification of the body of Christ.

Most of us will receive the first gift, but very few of us will receive the second.

The gift for the individual could more appropriately be called a prayer-and-praise language, for that is its primary purpose (1 Corinthians 14:4). When one's English words seem to run out, and one does not know what more to say in praise or in petition, then the Spirit takes over (by consent, always) and prays according to the will of God (Romans 8:26-27).

The gift for the body of Christ is to be used only when there is an interpreter, a person who has been given the gift of explaining in English the meaning of what has just been said. This gift is for the upbuilding of the church, for the edification of believers (1 Corinthians 14:26).

To avoid confusion, we were instructed clearly that if anyone felt led to use this latter gift in these meetings he was to come to the platform and "check out" with a designated person (who had received the gift of discernment) so that all things could be done orderly and in the will of God.

Pastor Mjorud then did something I'd never seen before in my thirty years of attending conferences and religious meetings. He gave an invitation to accept Christ as Savior during the first ten minutes of each service—instead of at the close of the service. He explained that although Lutherans had been confirmed, many had never experienced the baptism of John (which is the new birth). In order to prepare them to become candidates for the baptism of Jesus (which is by the Holy Spirit) he asked, "Would all who wish to receive the new birth please stand up, just where you are, and be prayed for."

People stood everywhere, right at their seats. Pastor Mjorud then prayed a simple prayer of acceptance, asking them to repeat it line by line. In fact, he asked all of us to repeat it together, "Because some of you sitting there should have been standing."

His prayer was something like this:

Prayer of Acceptance

Lord Jesus, I want to accept You as my personal Savior and receive the new birth. I confess I am a sinner and I need You as my Savior. Forgive all my sins and wash me clean in

*the blood of the Lamb. Thank You for hearing
my prayer. Amen.*

Things Seemed Clearer

Attending this conference cleared up a number of
things for me. I saw that Jesus Christ is the baptizer
(Mark 1:6-8) who imparts the Holy Spirit to those
who ask. I was confirmed in the belief I already had,
that wholehearted commitment to Christ is a
necessary condition, and that all gifts given to an
individual were for ministry, for the healing and the
upbuilding of the body of Christ.

That last phrase, the body of Christ, began to have
new meaning for me. I took special note that in this
conference the centrality of Christ was always
stressed, and this reassured me on this whole
"charismatic renewal," because my life and my
ministry has always been a Christ-centered one
(John 16:7-15).

I was also confirmed in my personal belief that the
Holy Spirit had already been given to me.

However, questions were still coming about the
difference between the *filling* of the Spirit and the
baptism of the Spirit. How the enemy uses
definitions and words to keep God's people
separated! Because of my early "holiness church"
background, these two terms seemed very
important to me, and still needed to be defined,

24

both in my mind and from the Scriptures.

Lutherans in Fresno, California

Sometime after the above experience, I was invited to Fresno, California, by a certain Lutheran church. A group of women from that church had heard me in a conference in their state where (very quietly) they had received the baptism of the Spirit from the teaching and laying on of hands by several faithful brethren.

Now their faith reached out to the extent of inviting a non-Lutheran woman (me) to their parish to teach conversational prayer, in the hopes that many of the husbands would be touched by God's Spirit by means of the low-key teaching ministry given to me. Their prayers were answered in many instances, all thanks be to God.

Then the confrontation came. The axe fell again. Shortly after my arrival I was asked point-blank: "Ros, have you received the baptism of the Spirit?"

I explained (it seemed I was always explaining in those days) that I had received *the filling* of the Spirit. They seemed satisfied with that until someone asked, "Did the Lord give you a prayer language at that time?"

When I told them He had not, they were eager to tell me, one after another, the blessings and joy which had come into their lives through that experience. Listening carefully, it seemed to me that they had been converted and sanctified (two terms used by our denomination) all at the same time, instead of two different experiences.

(Dear Lord, thank You for finally delivering me from trying to fit people into my religious category!)

There was such love among them, such evident leading of the Spirit, such love for Jesus Christ, that I loved them dearly. When they called me one morning and told me they would like to come to my hotel room and pray for me to receive the baptism and the gift of tongues, what could I say? I told them to come.

Thinking about their coming, praying about the whole subject and being a little nervous, I finally remember praying: "Lord, I am willing for all You have for me, and if You want to give me this 'questionable' gift through my Lutheran friends, I'm ready."

I also remember asking the Lord: "When they lay hands on me and pray for me, what should I be thinking? Where should my thoughts be?"

The answer came from the Voice I know so well: "Keep your heart stayed on Me, Jesus, and your inner eyes on the love-wounds in My hands, and give Me praise."

So they came. We knelt and prayed and there was much rejoicing and giving of thanks and praise. I did just what I had been told to do in my secret prayer time. There was great joy, many tears, and yet no gift of a prayer language was given to me.

The women seemed satisfied.

"It will come," they predicted, "it will come, because there was joy and freedom to pray, and the presence of our risen Lord is with us."

"Just wait . . . and expect it," another said.

Still another gave me her good word: "My prayer language came after I got home and was just looking out of the window. . . ."

Another said, "And mine came when I was singing in the shower."

They left and, of course, I immediately looked out of the window for a few moments! Then I sang in the shower! But nothing came and nothing happened.

I must admit that I was relieved and looked to Jesus who is always near me and with me and within me.

"Lord Jesus, You are enough for me.

"I don't have to have this gift, or any gift, unless I'm ready and it's Your time to give it to me.

You, yourself, are enough for me."

And He was.

It was true.

Jesus Christ is enough.

Dear Reader,

Your hang-ups or your prejudices or your religious background may be different than mine, but Jesus Christ is the same. And what He wants to give you is himself.

There is no fear in love.

It was at that Lutheran conference in Minneapolis that I first met the Reverend Dennis Bennett, Episcopal clergyman and author.[1] Since then I have met his wife, Rita, and have been a guest in their home near Seattle, as I have a married sister, Denise Adler, and a married brother, Bruce Rinker, living in that city and frequently visit them.

My sister, who had been Bible Study Fellowship teaching leader for ten years, was hospitalized about that time for lung and blood ailments. It looked like it was going to be a long hard siege. A nurse who knew Father Bennett saw him in the hospital corridor and told him Mrs. Adler was a patient there.

"I've been wanting to lay my hands on that woman for a long time," he said, and went right to her room and prayed for her. God touched her and she was home in a few days.

Later, Dennis and Rita spent a quiet afternoon at the Adlers', and at that time we all laid hands on Denise again for healing. Both of them used their

---

[1]Bennett, Dennis, *Nine O'clock in the Morning* (Plainfield, New Jersey: Logos International, 1970).

prayer language and Dennis looked at me and said, "Ros, use your prayer language."

What could I say? No time for explanations. For a moment I was tempted to just go ahead and pray in Chinese, as I often did: Who would know the difference? But I didn't. Instead I said honestly, "I don't have one yet."

Reflecting on that experience, I found I *did* want a prayer language to minister to others, but mixed into that desire was also my pride—wanting to be accepted by two people whom I loved and respected. As the months went on, I found there was more, a great deal more, of Ros Rinker that needed to be dealt with, admitted and handed over to Jesus.

Question: Why is it so easy for some to receive this gift and so hard for others?

Answer: Someone told me, to my chagrin, that the more independent one was, the harder it was.

My child, I would feed you with
the choicest foods,
And satisfy you with honey for
the taking.[2]

---

[2]Psalm 81:16, paraphrased.

Chapter Three

The Baptism of the Spirit

I was attending a Faith/at/Work conference held in Detroit, Michigan, at a certain Methodist church. At that time I already had several books in print and my public ministry was growing rapidly. The Lord was taking me through a cleansing and pruning period which brought deep inner anguish and mental suffering.

I needed someone to pray with me. You see, I believe Matthew 18:19, that when two people pray together there is power.

I looked around. "Lord, whom shall I ask?"

Then I saw Harold Hill[1] and simultaneously as I remembered past contacts with him, the inner instructions came. "Ask him, he loves Me." I remember Harold once saying, "If Jesus tells me

---

[1]Author of *How to Live Like a King's Kid* (Plainfield, New Jersey: Logos International, 1974) and several other titles.

31

black is white, I'll say 'Okay, Jesus, until You tell me differently.' "

We left the dining room and went into an adjoining classroom separated by one of those accordion-pleated room dividers. Harold brought a Canadian brother with him. I sat down, and they laid hands on me and prayed for me.

It was two years later at another FAW conference before I met him again. As we walked down the road together, he said, "Ros, come on over to my hotel. There are two Princeton Seminary fellows who want to receive the baptism."

"Sure," I replied, and then added, "but you know, Harold, I've never received this baptism myself, though I don't have any prejudice against it."

I'll never forget how he stopped dead in his tracks, turned and looked at me.

"Have you forgotten the time I prayed for you in Detroit?"

"I certainly have not."

"Well, what do you remember?"

I considered a moment. "I remember asking you to pray for me, and I remember breaking into tears—"

"What else do you remember?" he asked.

"Nothing—oh, yes, I remember reaching for a Kleenex from my purse on the floor, and then thinking, 'Never mind if they see me cry.' "

"Is that all?" Harold persisted. I wondered what

he was getting at, and assured him that *was* all I remembered. He looked thoughtful for a moment and finally said, "Well, you are the second one."

"The second . . . what?" What was he talking about!

"The second person I know who, when the Holy Spirit came upon you, spoke in tongues and didn't hear yourself."

I couldn't believe my ears. I questioned him again.

"You took off and spoke fluently in one of the most beautiful prayer languages I ever heard. That was a powerful anointing!"

I stood speechless.

I had heard nothing. Nothing at all.

The first thought which came to my mind was: Isn't God wonderful! And isn't He wise! He gave me this gift and I've been reaping all the benefits, and never called it by name! Thank You, Jesus. Thank You, Father.

Then another thought struck me: I wonder how many times this has happened to me in my own personal devotions?

And it could happen to you, dear reader, couldn't it?

Further Reflections

So, now what?

Well, I smiled to myself a great deal during those first weeks as I thought of various things:

No one could ever try to pattern after my experience.

I belonged. I really belonged to these dear Spirit-baptized people who love Jesus so much, and have such power to minister to others.

Yes, I was a "charismatic" and had received the gift of tongues without having to specifically seek. Why, I wondered, did the Lord choose that way for me? I'm sure He knew I was ready, and that I have always wanted to love Him best of all.

As I thought of these things and especially that I couldn't tell anyone to do what I did in order to receive this gift, it came to me: This is the way our Lord wants it. Each one of us must find our own way to the fullness of His Spirit, to receiving His gifts. He is always ready when we are.

Truthfully, I can't say that I wrote or spoke with any more power or unction after knowing that I'd spoken in tongues than I did before. It did seem that I was able to speak more authentically about the unconditional love of God, and my hearers accepted it.

Again and again, people have said, "I never realized nor believed God loved me until you told me. His love just seems to pour out of you when you speak."

But one thing was missing.

34

Not having known about my prayer language for these years, I had not been using it. Would the Lord ever give it back to me?

Chapter Four

God's Gifts
Cannot Be Programmed

Speaking at a CFO (Camp Farthest Out) conference in Iowa, I shared the platform with the Reverend Alfred L. Durrance, rector of Grace Episcopal Church in Ocala, Florida. Al and Julie and their four sons have since become good friends of mine during several visits to Florida in the past few years.

At the conference, the re-education of Ros Rinker regarding the Holy Spirit continued. One afternoon, by special request of the campers, Father Al spent three hours taking us through the whole Bible on the subject of the Holy Spirit—right down to the present day.

"Why haven't I heard this before?" I asked myself. So many things were cleared up for me that day. I found my heart and mind enlightened and strengthened. I had put the subject of the Holy Spirit on the lay-away shelf for fourteen years during the time I was a student counselor, because I didn't know what to do about it—or Him. I turned my attention to two other pressing subjects because students needed them: the deity of our Lord and the meaning of His atonement. Both of these subjects brought stability to my own faith, and at the same time developed the gift of teaching which was becoming apparent.

"Someday, in God's time, I'll know more about the Holy Spirit," I remember having said, for I never minimized His importance in the life of a believer. But in my wildest dreams I never imagined it would be an Episcopal clergyman who would enlighten me. The healing of my prejudices was taking place and I knew it.

It was exciting. What next?

At this same conference I met a well-meaning person who attempted to hasten God's program for me.

After one of my teaching sessions a small woman approached me before I left the platform.

"You have received the baptism of the Holy Spirit, haven't you?"

"Yes, I have." I could say it truthfully now.

"I was sure you had, because of the authority with

which you speak." She paused for a moment and then asked, "Did you speak in a tongue?"

"Yes, I did," I answered, "and tell me who you are."

She told me her name and that she was an ordained pentecostal minister. But she had another question.

"And are you using that prayer language every day?"

I had to admit I was not.

"Well, you should, because the Spirit can pray through you and greatly increase your ministry."

It was time I told her what actually happened, so we sat down and I shared with her what I've already related in the last chapter.

This interested lady assured me that because I had once received the prayer language, it could be renewed. She laid hands on me and prayed earnestly. I was wide open by this time, with no holds barred, but nothing happened, no sounds came.

A similar experience to this happened two more times during the next year, when others urged me to recover the prayer language, and both times not a thing happened. On one occasion, several persons attempted to "cast out demons" of silence (or whatever) and the Counselor within me said, "That's enough; tell them you are ready to obey and please Me." I quietly did so, got up and left, wondering about the whole process.

After that, the Lord Jesus seemed to be very near to me. He seemed to say, "Am I not enough for you? Seek Me, and Me alone. Are you not satisfied with the gifts I have already given to you?"

"Yes, Lord," I answered, for my heart continually was saying, "Ask me, Lord, I want to say yes."

He continued, "Do you think you can choose your own gift? You know the precious gift of the Holy Spirit is already yours. Any other gift will be chosen for you, and will be given to you in My own time. It will be for your edification and for the building up of My body on earth."

My Reflections

All these rather contrived experiences at the hands of well-meaning persons gave me an understanding of why so many are skeptical of the baptism of the Spirit. By this time I wondered if the prayer language was the primary sign or test of having received the Holy Spirit. (We will further discuss this in a coming chapter.) For some it may be the valid sign, but is it for all?

I was becoming aware of the great need for teaching among those who have received this baptism and who try to urge it upon others without guidance. I am convinced, as I have already said, that we cannot pigeonhole the Holy Spirit and tell Him how and when to come to us, but I believe that all the gifts are available to us in time of need.

To the thirsty, Jesus promised, will the Spirit be given, like a free-flowing river of living water (John 7:38-39). After that these same persons will have power to speak and to testify of Jesus and His gospel (Acts 1:8).

My prayer, then, was like this: "Lord Jesus, my heart says yes to all You want to give me. Prepare my heart. Send people, or books, or circumstances which will increase my thirst and expectation. Forgive me when I become impatient, and make me ready to receive any gift You have for me."

In the meantime, I continued to accept invitations and to conduct prayer workshops in many states and abroad, and marveled at the free flow of teaching which came through me to others. A quiet patience possessed me, and I was willing to wait for God's own time to give me back my prayer language.

Chapter Five

A Methodist Conference in Florida

The following report[1] could have been at the end of this chapter, but it is placed here as a testimony to the power of God because of answered prayer:

"The Second Annual Conference on Victorious Living sponsored by The Methodist Hour Radio Network was hailed as a tremendous success by over 200 registrants from over 20 states. The theme of this year's conference, 'What the Holy Spirit is doing in the church today,' was introduced by Methodist Hour speaker, Rev. Herbert Bowdoin as the three-day conference got under way at Baptist Assembly Grounds at Lake Yale, Florida on February 26, 1975.

"Highlights of the conference centered around the moving expository preaching of Rev. Roy

[1]From "Quarterly," Vol. 1, No. 4, June, July, August 1975 (Jacksonville, Florida).

Putman, minister of Trinity United Methodist
Church of Greensboro, N.C., and the exciting
moving spirit of Miss Rosalind Rinker, gifted author
and lecturer on prayer. Miss Rinker, on the last day
of the conference, urged that a spirit of love prevail
as charismatics and non-charismatics move together
in the great move of the Holy Spirit in and out of the
church today.

"Following Miss Rinker's message the anointing
of the Holy Spirit was so great that nearly the entire
gathering were standing with arms raised in worship
of Jesus as they were led in praise of the King of kings
by Jimmy Smith, singer and pianist of the Methodist
Hour Staff."

The Beforehand Story

The invitation to take part in this conference gave
me another opportunity to say "Yes, Lord." A full
program had already been set up for Florida, and
this invitation came by telephone while I was still in
my home in California. To add another engagement
meant using some of the time allocated to rest.

Now one of the instructions the Lord gave to me
when I started this teaching ministry was "Get
enough rest. . . . Be rested, then my Spirit can flow
through you." By experience I have proved this to
be true. As I inquired about His will in this situation,
I felt I should accept.

Julie Durrance drove me to the conference, but she was unable to stay. As I remember it was almost a two-hour drive. There were periods of silence as we drove, in which I was quietly committing the coming days into the Lord's hands.

Then Julie spoke. "Ros, there's something troubling you, isn't there? Can I help? I could pray."

I looked at her in astonishment, for I had not breathed a word of my misgivings about that conference. The very title, "Victorious Life," had made me hesitant to accept the invitation. This attitude stemmed back to my twenties and thirties, when I earnestly sought to be a victorious Christian, and followed several schools of teaching on Christian perfection. (This story is told in *Within the Circle.*)

One of them was this "victorious life" teaching. Briefly, they taught that man has two natures (see Romans 6 and 7) and to make the spiritual nature strong, one should starve the fleshly or sinful nature. I remember an illustration they used: The master had a black dog and a white dog. He should starve the black one and feed the white one. It seemed to me that in the end it was a matter of performance rather than of faith, and I found no adequate or workable help.

Real spiritual growth and stability came to me in the Lord's timing, first through that in-depth study I'd made of the atonement and the deity of our Lord; and second through the books of Norman Grubb on the union life of the believer with his Lord.[2]

With the above explanation, perhaps you can understand some of the thoughts coming to me as I faced this conference. Were they going to teach "the victorious life"? The same old line of thought? Were they charismatic, Spirit-filled people? Or "holiness"? What emphasis did they have? Would my message fit into their program? "Lord, make me sensitive to Your will and give me Your message."

Did Julie sense these apprehensive questions?

"How did you know I was troubled?" I asked.

"Oh," she tossed her head and smiled as she drove on, "sometimes the Lord gives me the gift of discernment and when He does, I obey Him."

Once again the teaching I give to others came back to help me. "If two of you shall agree on earth as touching any thing that they shall ask, it shall be done for them of my Father in heaven" (Matthew 18:19 KJV). I really count on that promise and practice it.

I shared with her the thoughts I had been thinking, and she said, "The enemy is trying to disqualify you by fear and doubt, but Jesus is stronger. When we get to the conference grounds and find your room, I'll lay hands on you and pray for deliverance from those old oppressions, and ask for a new anointing for the next two days."

So this Episcopalian rector's wife taught me the spiritual value of using the gifts given to her by the

---

[2]Grubb, Norman, *God Unlimited* and *The Spontaneous You* (Fort Washington, Pennsylvania: Christian Literature Crusade, 1966).

Holy Spirit: the laying on of hands, the rebuking of Satan, and the importance of taking the freedom promised to us. Together we gave thanks and praise for the coming release and the answers.

First of all, the uneasiness left me. I was able to move among the people, love them, care about them, to forget the past, including all judgmental thoughts. Furthermore, my speaking sessions were filled with freedom and freshness.

Let me share how Jesus began to lead me. I prayed, "Lord, show me what to speak on at each one of these two services."

The answer came. The first evening I was to teach them to pray together, using conversational (or dialogue) prayer in small groups—with simplicity and honesty, like children in Jesus' presence; with praise and thanksgiving; with instruction on personal confession and how to give absolution to the confessor; closing with effective ways of intercession.

The second meeting, which was the last session of the conference, was something else. I trembled to think of what Jesus was asking me to do: speak on my observations at that conference, and also of His will for love and unity among His children.

What were my observations?

There was a huge lounge, one end of whch had

been ultilized as a bookstore, well stocked with a person in charge full time. I visited it, took time to inform myself about the nature of books they had selected, and sat down to glance through several.

Very soon my attention was drawn to the other end of the room. There in front of a fireplace stood two tables, end to end, with a few books and some literature displayed.

I went over to investigate, and to my surprise realized that Methodism has a charismatic branch of believers! But there was no person in charge, only a cardboard box in which to deposit cash for anything one might purchase. I selected several things and left the money. From time to time, I purposely went through the lounge, hoping to see someone at that table with whom I could speak. I never saw anyone there. The table stood alone and lonely.

So, I thought to myself, the Spirit-baptized Methodists are here, but seemingly not very welcome, and certainly not in evidence. In view of the "new wind blowing" through the liturgical churches which I had seen personally, I asked myself: What does God want to do for the Methodist church in Florida? And particularly at this conference?

Keeping my ears open, I further observed that none of the messages given in the main services (nor the workshops I was able to attend) taught the Spirit-filled life or even touched on the wonderful phenomena going on in the body of Christ today. That is, the miracle of God's Holy Spirit being poured out upon all flesh, resulting in the love, unity and healing of God's people—especially among denominations previously separated by doctrine and/or prejudice.

Briefly, my message[3] contained my own testimony and a few almost unbelievable stories of changed lives and new ministries given to priests and sisters of the Roman Catholic church, through the teaching and practice of conversational prayer.

I also told what I'd observed about the two book tables in the lounge, and closed with an exhortation from the seventeenth chapter of John's Gospel, which reminds us that our Lord prayed for unity and love among His children, and challenged them to lay down all judgmental opinions, and to love and to forgive one another.

In closing, I suggested that we follow the example of our Catholic and Episcopal brothers—"pass the peace"—and I demonstrated it right there. Immediately the whole floor was a beautiful scene of brothers and sisters with arms around each other, forgiving one another with tears of joy.

Giving the Peace: "The peace of the Lord be with you."

The Response: "And also with you."

---

[3]Printed in full in "Quarterly," ibid., pp. 19-27.

Thank You, Jesus, for asking me to go.
Thank You for giving me freedom through Julie
to be Your channel.
Thank You for Julie, and her faithfulness in
using the gifts You gave her.
Ask me, Lord, I want to say yes.

Chapter Six

God's Gift
Given in Praise

It was through the quiet influence of my good friends, Al and Julie Durrance, that God finally removed the last of my excuses, filled my heart and mouth with His praises, and returned to me the gift of a prayer language.

My first invitation to Florida came after that Iowa conference, when Father Al invited me to Grace Episcopal in Ocala. Other invitations followed, and for a period of four consecutive years I held workshops in the Central Episcopal Diocese of Florida.

This diocese has a predominance of Spirit-baptized priests, probably due to the fact that their bishop, The Right Reverend James Folwell, is charismatic. I learned many good and helpful things concerning life in the Spirit and the gifts of the Spirit from my Episcopal brothers and sisters.

I had already been confirmed an Episcopalian six years before the events of chapters five and six, * and will tell you about that in chapter seven. However, I want to keep the sequence of my story regarding saying, "Yes, Lord," on this particular issue.

Continued contact with these Spirit-filled people gave me an entirely new picture of what it means to belong to a community of loving sons and daughters of God who exercise the gifts of the Spirit in a local church, thus ministering to each other, whether or not they agree totally about the "charismatic renewal" going on in their midst.

I must admit that, from the events of chapter four when misguided but zealous persons tried to help me, I was secretly glad that I didn't possess that controversial gift of tongues, but on the other hand I was happy to be identified as a member of this loving community. It was enough that I had once been given that gift, but I was not totally convinced that I needed it, or just how it was to be used.

Little did I ever dream that the Florida Episcopalians were to be God's channel to renew that gift. Two events contributed to that renewal.

I have already written of the first in Chapter five, regarding the ministry of my friend Julie Durrance at the time of that Methodist conference. Her discernment and intercession for me at that

*Fourteen years at this writing.

52

particular time of need made a deep impression on me. My heart and mind were opening up, and I was being prepared for the next event.

A task force of twelve clergy and lay persons, led by Harry Griffith of the Bible Reading Fellowship of the Episcopal Church, invited me to meet with them for one week—as they put it, "to pick my brains" on the subject of how Episcopalians could become witnesses for Jesus Christ. What new things God is doing!

The openness and unity of that group was something I'd never experienced before. By the second day we were sharing our personal needs and praying for one another in a healing spirit of love. Here I was exposed to Spirit-filled Episcopalians who were already exercising varied gifts of the Spirit in ministry to one another. Again, I was deeply impressed, and God used these dear ones to create in me more desire for the gifts of the Spirit, particularly the prayer language of praise.

Another result of that week was a new book, *Sharing God's Love*, co-edited by Harry and myself,[1] which explored seven different kinds of people one might find in an Episcopal (or any) church.

Two Bouquets of Praise

The importance of regular times of praise and thanksgiving came to me through contact with

---

[1] Rinker, Rosalind, and Griffith, Harry (Grand Rapids, Michigan: Zondervan, 1976).

Florida friends, and so again the renewal of my prayer language began to be a current subject between Jesus and me. No one questioned me on this subject, and I stopped talking about it to others.

I felt led to offer praise to Jesus Christ, my Lord, three times daily as an act of devotion—morning, noon, and night. I spent fifteen minutes doing nothing but offering praise and thanksgiving (with no petitions at all) to God, the Father, Son, and Holy Spirit.

It was a blessed time, which I began to look forward to. Soon I found myself offering this daily praise somewhat like a bouquet of flowers, using all the phrases I knew from the psalms, the hymnal, the Eucharist, and my own heart. The first thing I knew there were two bouquets!

The first was in English, and the second was in Chinese, growing, as it were, out of the first with all the Chinese prayer words I remembered.

Surely now, I said to myself, during this prayer time of praise the gift would be renewed. But time went on and I found I was offering that praise time as a sort of exchange! I would offer praise, and God would give my prayer language back to me. But no such thing happened.

As I grew aware that it was not happening, I was disappointed. His voice seemed to come to me again: "Am I not enough for you? Are not the gifts I have already given you enough? Do you still need one more just because others have received it?"

My first answer was, "No, I don't need another gift, but I would like it."

My second answer was, "Yes, Lord, You are enough."

He was teaching me the importance of seeking Him first. To depend upon Him alone, not His gifts. His presence is more to be desired than all His gifts.

So I quietly continued my praise and thanksgiving times, just because of His love for me and mine for Him, and because *He is enough*. It seems that this is a test which frequently reoccurs in my life and always on a different subject. So subtle is my heart, and so patient is my Lord who knows the real intent of that heart.

The Miracle of that Third Bouquet

And then one day, when I was not even expecting it, not looking for it, the blessed gift was given! I offered Him my bouquet of English praise, and then of Chinese praise, and quietly a third bouquet of praise was there: A beautiful prayer language was pouring out of my lips, a language of love and praise.

I stopped and laughed aloud with joy! Would it still be there if I stopped? Sure enough, I could start and stop it at will, and the rest of the day I went around in a glorious celebration! And I didn't have to look out of the window, or sing in the shower!

In the loving-kindness of God's perfect timing, He had purified my motives, and given me a prayer language in which to praise Him, which saturated me, filled me, and brought sweet healing to every hurt place.

It was such a beautiful, kind of private and personal thing between Jesus and me, that I didn't tell anyone for quite a while. When I did, there was even more rejoicing. It took me a long time to know how to use this gift in other ways, but I will share some of that with you later in this book.

Thanks be to God for His beautiful gifts to the children of men!

A prayer for you who are still seeking:

Since You, O Lord,
> know all things, let me relax into quiet thanksgiving at Your feet, and stop trying to receive the esoteric gift given to those who love You, or who are destined to love You. Teach me not to look to people, but to look to You, Lord Jesus, for You are the baptizer. I will wait and give praise to You and love You, satisfied with yourself alone.
>> Amen.

Chapter Seven

A New Church Home

I grew up, the oldest of six, in a small North Dakota town called New Rockford, where my mother had been the high school principal and my father was an attorney. We attended the Methodist Episcopal church every Sunday and always sat in the same pew on the left-hand side. I never knew what "Episcopal" meant until much later, but little did I ever dream that God would prepare me for a ministry in that denomination, in which, for the first time in my adult life, I would find a loving church home.

During my teens I had membership also in the Church of the Nazarene; then in later years in the Presbyterian church. And now, for the past fourteen years, my membership has been in the Episcopal church.

These changes were accompanied by some change in theology and/or locale and served to acquaint me with both sides of the theological fence.[1] This gave me a fine chance to say another yes to the Lord, when it came to freedom from prejudice and in withholding judgmental opinions.

God never gives His children the blueprint ahead of time. He asks for trust and obedience, and for commitment to His way—all based on His unconditional love. Being very human, this is not an easy way to follow and I often try to outguess Him and ascertain what He has in mind. But it doesn't work. Believe me, it doesn't work.

I do know, from walking with Him through the years, that His way is always best and that it is a day-to-day walk with Jesus, doing the best I can in the here-and-now. I have learned to leave both the results and the outcome to His mercy and kindness. One thing I need to keep reminding myself is that when I fail He is a great Redeemer, and not only redeems my mistakes, He even uses the very failure to show me His love.

The Episcopal Church in Honolulu

My decision to store my belongings and move to Honolulu for a few years came because of a needed change and because of a severe conflict which I was

---

[1]My autobiography in length is in *Within the Circle* (Grand Rapids, Michigan: Zondervan, 1973).

unable to resolve. My sister, Denise, knew a family who needed a house-sitter for the summer, so I applied and was accepted. Later I rented an apartment and stayed for three years.

During that time the Lord opened many doors for ministry and teaching; my seventh book, *Praying Together*, was written there.[2]

Through a mutual friend, I was soon introduced to Jean Potter, a transplanted New Zealander, who promptly invited me to attend the Episcopal chapel on the second floor of the Reef Hotel, "Because we need help greeting all the tourists on the terrace after the service."

A small event which made me feel very welcome occurred that next Sunday as I entered the hall where the chapel was located. There was a lady sitting at a card table greeting visitors and making out name cards.

"Oh, I've been waiting for you, Ros Rinker. Jane Adams, the vicar's wife, couldn't be here today, but she would like you to autograph her books."

There on the table lay three or four of my books, well read and marked up. I knew at once I was going to like that chapel!

My previous contact with the Episcopal church had been largely limited to admiring lovely old church buildings. I had, on occasion, gone to a few early morning Eucharists with Faith/at/Work friends—Louise Mohr, Gert Behanna, Bertha

[2]See Rinker, Rosalind, *Praying Together* (Grand Rapids, Michigan: Zondervan, 1968).

Elliott and others. The Eucharist, as celebrated by liturgical churches, became a time of special nearness to Christ for me. My heart is always touched, refreshed and drawn out in deep worship. Think of it: A whole half hour of quiet meditation on Jesus Christ, His Person and His Work!

I soon began to attend the Wednesday morning Eucharists at the chapel and found much comfort and healing in that simple yet profound celebration. God took me all the way to Honolulu to be able to help me once more to say yes to Him on several issues. Not that I was deliberately refusing: I was in a state of confusion in which my own personal desires conflicted with His will for me.

Rev. Stanley E. Adams, retired major from the Marine Corps, was vicar, and I soon found myself staying to chat with him after that Wednesday morning Eucharist.

One day he came up with, "How about doing something for us on a Monday night? We don't have too much going for us here. Why not try something?"

I was already teaching a large class of military wives at Hickam Air Force Base once a week, so it was not long before young airmen and airwomen who worked during the day found out about that Monday evening class and began to bring their friends. While teaching them to pray and to know Christ, I centered on His love for them and our love for each other. The first thing I knew they were calling that meeting "Ros's Love-in"!

Father Adams came to a few of my sessions and then one day asked me to come to a class he was teaching. It turned out to be a confirmation class! And I had a decision to make. I'll admit I was a bit troubled. Here I was writing books and teaching a very unstructured dialogue-type of prayer (called conversational prayer). Should I join a church which (I thought then) used only a structured prayer book?

"Lord, guide me. Show me what to do. Are you speaking to me? Ask me, Lord, I want to say yes to Your will."

I felt the need to talk and pray with someone who loved Jesus, and made a luncheon appointment with Mrs. C. That very morning while I was laying the matter before Him, He gave me His answer. I was telling Him both sides of the situation and as I talked was aware that I was gesturing with my hands as well.

"Lord, on the one hand . . . and then on the other. . . ." As I spoke, suddenly I remembered Tevye, the Jewish Russian farmer who talked like that to the Lord Who was always present. I, too, became very aware that He was present.

"You have two hands, don't you? You need them both, don't you? What about two kinds of prayer: liturgical prayer and conversational prayer? They both meet a need in your life, don't they?"

A light was turned on. I began to give thanks and praise. Once more I had said yes to His will, and great peace filled my heart and my mind. I joined the confirmation class and was duly confirmed by Bishop Kennedy.

At present, I am a member of St. James Episcopal Church of Newport Beach. It happened like this: Four years ago I was invited to give them a prayer workshop, and a year later Betty Connelly, who became one of my best friends, invited me to pray about joining their church. I have never known such warm, loving, unjudgmental people. Our priest, The Reverend John P. Ashey, II, received the Holy Spirit before his people did, and has led three *Life in the Spirit* classes of some seventy-five persons each time. The renewal is going on, and we are working together to discover how our lay people can find and use their gifts to build up the body of Christ.

Due to the nature of my work as a traveling counselor when I was in student work, I have never really belonged to a local congregation. Now I am enjoying the love and prayers of God's people at St. James, and some deep and lasting friendships have been made.

PART II:

The Gift of a Prayer Language

Chapter Eight

How Important
Is This Gift?

If we are to assume that the list of gifts given by St. Paul in chapter twelve of 1 Corinthians is according to their importance, then we must assume that the gift of speaking in an unknown tongue is not one of prime importance, because it is the very last one he mentions.

However, when we begin to look at the purpose of these gifts, we find it is the same Spirit who produces all of them, and who distributes them to each individual as He will. Paul goes on to compare the church of Christ to the human body, where each member functioning properly enables the whole body to grow—to mature in love (1 Corinthians 12:4, 5, 11, 25).

Since each member of that body is important and

no single one is indispensable, it follows that each gift is equally important. Therefore, we conclude that the gift of tongues is one of significant worth, and not to be ignored or despised.

Why do we not get more teaching on this subject of gifts of the Spirit, including the gift of tongues? Particularly since the purpose for believers receiving gifts is that for which we all deeply long: growth and maturity in love. Is fear such a big factor that we are unable to face truth?

The 64-dollar question which seems to plague people, "Do I *have to* speak in tongues," can be answered with a simple, "No, you do not have to."

Someone heard David du Plessis answer that question with, "No, you don't have to—but you probably will."

The following passages make it very plain that while all of the gifts are important, no one believer possesses all of them.

In the King James Version, twelfth chapter of 1 Corinthians, verses 29 and 30, the translators have used rhetorical questions, which in this instance means asking a question with an obviously negative answer. (Italics are mine.)

Are all apostles? (*no*) are all prophets? (*no*) are all teachers? (*no*) are all workers of miracles? (*no*) Have all the gifts of healing? (*no*) do all speak with tongues? (*no*) do all interpret? (*no*)

The American Bible Society (Today's English Version) gives these same verses in this more easily understood form:

They are not all apostles or prophets or teachers. Not everyone has the power to work miracles or to heal diseases or to speak in strange tongues or to explain what is said.

The question I'd like to ask you is: "Would a loving God give you a gift unsuited to you personally?"

The prime question for you to ask yourself is: "Am I open to receive any gift the Holy Spirit wants to give me?"

I would like to ask you, my brothers and sisters, to lay aside your own prejudices, either for or against, and take another look at the gentle way in which the Spirit leads God's children to love Jesus.

As I look back on the years I have written about, I am amazed at the goodness of God, who gave me His Holy Spirit in spite of my "taught and programmed prejudices." One thing I am sure of, He will never ask more of you than you are able to receive. And when you are unable to see clearly some truth which is important to Him, He will patiently guide you and change you until you can see clearly.

Because He loves you very much.

Chapter Nine

What Is the Purpose of This Gift?

Because it is a controversial subject, one which easily arouses defenses and affronts the pride of man by its very mystery and simplicity, it is necessary for us to clearly define and understand the purpose of this gift of prayer language (i.e., tongues/glossolalia).

In this chapter we will look at the events of the day of Pentecost and the purpose of the gift of tongues at that time. We will also examine the purpose of that gift in the church today. In the next chapter we will go into the benefits (or purpose) of this gift in our individual lives.

The Day of Pentecost

The first gift of tongues was on the day of

Pentecost (Acts 2), when every man heard the message of the risen Christ in his own language. So *tongues* on that occasion were in known languages, and the purpose was twofold: to evangelize the unbelievers and to unite believers.

In our churches today, the gift of tongues does two things. It amazingly unites persons of denominations who previously seemed to have little in common. And secondly, it has been known to become a divisive factor when love is absent and prejudice is present, which is true of any gift exercised by the possessor.

Do people speak in known languages today as a result of the baptism of the Holy Spirit?

Yes, there have been instances reported, but they seem to be only for a specific time, or for a specific person. Both Catherine Marshall and Dennis Bennett report such happenings.[1]

I recall the story of two missionaries who believed God would give them the Chinese language without studying it. They lived near the inland city of Paotingfu, Hopei Province, where some of my friends lived, and that is how I knew about them. For two years they prayed and fasted that the Chinese language would be given to them as a gift. Finally they gave up, hired a teacher and learned to speak Chinese like the rest of us by application and hard work.

Therefore, we can conclude the general

---

[1]Bennett, Dennis and Rita, *The Holy Spirit and You* (Plainfield, New Jersey: Logos International, 1971), chapter 7. Marshall, Catherine, *The Helper* (Waco, Texas: Chosen Books, 1978), chapter 7.

experience of those baptized with the Holy Spirit today is that they do not receive a known language, but an unknown one, a heavenly language, the purpose of which we will consider next.

In the Church Today

What practical benefits does the gift of tongues, or the prayer language, have in the church today?

First, when the gift is practiced by individuals, it brings the presence of Jesus very near, which in turn brings personal enrichment, comfort, and guidance to their own lives and thus influences the whole church.

Second, when this gift is practiced in the congregation audibly and is interpreted, it brings encouragement, love, forgiveness, consolation, knowledge, teaching, upbuilding, and often prophecy.

First Corinthians, 12th Chapter

In this chapter, St. Paul writes about the importance and use of all the gifts, calling attention to the fact that love, which is the fruit of the Spirit, is more important than all the gifts. The last verse of this chapter leads right into the "Love Chapter." He does teach that *prophecy* (which is forth-telling God's message) and *tongues* follow closely after love, but without love, they are nothing.

The definitions St. Paul gives, the explanations, the correction of abuses, the proper uses of these gifts are plainly written there for us to read, and to evaluate in our present setting. Some of the modern translations of the Bible help us gain a better understanding of what is actually being taught.

Ephesians, Chapter 4
Under the control of the Spirit all the different parts of the body fit together so when each part works as it should, the whole body grows and builds itself up in love. (Ephesians 4:16, paraphrase)

In other words, when all the gifts are in operation (when individuals are using them under the guidance of the Holy Spirit) there is growth and maturity. *There is freedom in giving love and forgiveness.* Thus we all become workers together, letting God do His work through us instead of trying to do it for Him.

Have I seen this love and forgiveness in operation? I'd like to tell you about just such an instance which took place in the Long Beach Arena in 1976, at the Southern California Roman Catholic Charismatic Conference.

One afternoon, Father John Bertolucci was giving us an excellent study of the seventeenth chapter of St. John, which is the high priestly prayer of our Lord:

I do not pray for these only, but also for those who believe in me through their word, that they may all be one; even as thou, Father, art in me, and I in thee . . . that the world may believe that thou hast sent me. . . . I in them and thou in me, that they may become perfectly one, so that the world may know that thou hast sent me and hast loved them even as thou hast loved me. (John 17:20-23 RSV)

Without warning, he suddenly asked those in the audience who were not Roman Catholics to please stand up. I turned to my friend, Elaine Reedy. "I don't want to stand up; I feel I *am* one of you." But I stood up. Then I looked around, and was disappointed at the few non-Catholics (Protestants) who were present to witness and to participate in the beautiful renewal which is going on in this great church.

The next request will almost blow your mind!

"I would like you, my Catholic brothers and sisters, to go to these standing brothers and sisters, and put your arms around them and say, 'Forgive me, my brother (my sister), for the way I have treated you, and the way our church has treated you.' "

Immediately a big man in front of me stood up, turned around, clasped me in his arms with tears running down his face, and apologized in those words. When he was through, I saw that no one was sitting in that great arena. There were lines of people behind every standing Protestant. There was a line almost a block long (or so it seemed) waiting for me!

Oh, the love which was poured out that day! Oh, the tears which were shed! And oh, the healing which came into all our hearts. Prejudice and apartness fled away, and love and forgiveness came to us that day! My prejudices were gone a long time ago, but I stood in proxy for Protestant friends whom I knew were still unable to cope with theirs.

Such an event could never have happened without the love of God "shed abroad in our hearts by the Holy Ghost which is given unto us" (Romans 5:5).

Someday, when God guides me, I'd like to repeat that love feast in the largely Protestant audiences where I usually speak.

The gift of tongues is only one of the gifts which the Roman Catholic church is using to the glory of God. The gift of prophecy and of discernment of spirits is also practiced in their charismatic Masses; words of comfort, of discipline, and of warning are given and interpreted into English. Thus the revival that many Protestants have been praying for is taking place, but few are aware how God is answering their prayers.

Thank God for the simplicity of obedience, which is given to childlike believers who are willing to ask for and receive all the gifts that God waits to give them.

Chapter Ten

What Purpose Does the Prayer Language Have in Our Personal Lives?

The story in the previous chapter brings joy to us, because of the beautiful things the Holy Spirit gives to us when we are obedient and when we let the fruits as well as the gifts of the Spirit flow through us.

In my own personal experience, I have discovered that offering praise to Jesus my Lord, to my heavenly Father, and to the blessed Comforter brings great release and joy into my whole being. Sometimes the prayer is one of personal enrichment and pure joy, other times it brings wisdom, or intercession, or deliverance, or even warning.

Because of the way in which my prayer language was given to me, I have continued daily to give praise in all three languages: English, Chinese, and the heavenly prayer language. As a result, my spirit is uplifted, I am comforted in times of distress or decision, I am assured of God's never-changing love for me. I go about my daily work knowing my life is totally in His hands, and that all He brings to me is in His will. I know that Jesus is with me, that He lives within me. I am His, His very own property. And my responsibility is to use all the common sense I was born with to take care of what belongs to Him.

For Healing

In my own church there is opportunity for laying-on-of-hands for any healing needed—after the morning Eucharist, at the altar, and at the Friday morning women's prayer group. As I pray for another, I do not always know what to pray for, and so quietly (under my breath) I use my prayer language and then wait and listen. During that time, a thought comes, which when expressed in English seems to bring the needed faith or blessing to my brother or sister.

Prayer of Authority

Jesus taught this in Mark 11:22-25. Speak to your mountain! Command it to disappear! Peter spoke the word of authority to the blind man at the gate called Beautiful in Acts 3:6, when he said, ". . . In the name of Jesus Christ of Nazareth, rise up and walk."

I do not claim to have a special gift of healing, but I believe that any Spirit-filled child of God may pray for healing when requested to do so, or when compassion moves deeply in his heart. On several occasions when I have been asked to pray for individuals and have done so with the authority of Jesus' Name, there has been healing—of cancer, spastic fibrosis, a twisted leg and rib cage, to name the more spectacular, as well as many minor ailments. Reading books like *Healing*, by Father Francis MacNutt, [1] and others, has strengthened my faith and courage to pray with authority when inner direction comes.

For Guidance

At first I did not know how to interpret the sounds (nor the feelings) given to me as I prayed in this heavenly language. Then Grace McCoy (one of my prayer partners) gave me a copy of Oral Roberts' *3 Most Important Steps to Your Better Health and Miracle Living*[2] and told me to be sure to read the seventh chapter. It was a surprise and revelation, because what I found in that chapter was just what was taking place in my own prayer life.

As I prayed "with my spirit" and continued to worship and give praise, a sudden thought in English would come. At first, I would push it out and

[1] MacNutt, Francis (Notre Dame, Indiana: Ave Maria Press, 1974).
[2] Roberts, Oral (Tulsa, Oklahoma: Oral Roberts Evangelistic Association, Inc., 1976).

continue my praise; then I began to think about that:
Could it be a message from the Lord while my mind
was quiet and receptive and my spirit was giving
thanks? So I recognized His voice, and was able to
receive what God was saying to me. As the book
explained, I was interpreting my own "tongues"
back to my understanding. (See 1 Corinthians
14:13-14.) How exciting it is, then, to be with Jesus
in prayer, and to experience all of this!

For Warning

On several occasions, I have been given different
prayer languages, with totally different sounds. I am
learning how to distinguish them, and to understand
for what purpose they are given. I continue to trust
the Holy Spirit to guide me, and to show me His will
and purpose.

I remember the first time this happened to me. A
call to prayer came, and as I drove to that address, I
prayed "in the Spirit" and was surprised at the jerky,
dissonant sounds that came out—not at all like the
smooth, harmonious prayer/praise sounds that
usually flow out. I was alerted at once, and sure
enough, there was just cause to be watchful. I
realized anew the importance of paying attention to
how the Holy Spirit is praying through me (see
Romans 8:26-27), as this prepares me for conflict
ahead, and also alerts me to the need for praying the

prayer of authority in Jesus' Name.

For Deliverance

I heard Jean Stone Willians speak during our Episcopal Charismatic Conference, 1978, and tell how individuals who prayed for half an hour "in the Spirit" had more power to deal with and deliver drug addicts than those who did not.

I thought I'd try it at home, praying half an hour in the Spirit; but perhaps not having any drug addicts to help, my praise time amounted to less than five minutes! I'll admit I'm still a beginner at learning to use the prayer language. But I practice it any time I want to: driving in the car, in an elevator when I'm alone, before I go to sleep, in my own private devotions, taking a walk, swimming in the pool, or any time at all—both in praise and in intercession.

Deliverance is usually used for the relief of some kind of oppression by evil and/or Satan, such as Father MacNutt outlines in his book, *Healing*: drugs, alcohol, perversions, the occult, evil spirits, etc. This is a special gift given to some people, and one to be used with great care and responsibility. Jesus delivered many from such oppression in His earthly ministry, and is carrying on that ministry through His followers today (John 14:12).

In concluding this chapter, I'd like to say again that "praying in the Spirit" brings the presence of

Jesus very near to me, and He is with me all day long
no matter what I'm doing. This is what is known as
"praying without ceasing."

His presence and anointing are especially with me
in meetings where I've been asked "please not to
bring any charismatic teaching," as well as those who
ask me to come and bring the message the Lord has
given me. I understand the panic and distress of the
former group, for I was in their shoes once.

God's timing is perfect and He will teach us all He
wants us to know in His own way and time. I have
observed that the low-key messages God gives me
do help break down barriers of tradition, fear, and
prejudice.

My prayer is always:
　　Ask me, Lord,
　　I want to say yes,
　　to whatever You are planning for me.

Father, You are filled
　　with life and power
　　while we are weak and in need.
We beg You now and every day
　　to fracture the power
　　of sin in our lives
and to flood us with the light
　　of Your love,
Who is Jesus Christ,

Who lives and rules with You,
And the Holy Spirit,
One God now and forever.

Amen.

Chapter Eleven

What Is the Valid Sign of Having Received the Baptism of the Spirit?

Teach me, Lord,
> I want to accept,
> I want to say yes.
Teach me Your ways.
> How do You want us to
> recognize each other
> as belonging to the
> same Family?

In chapter eight, we established the fact that there is no single gift which is of more importance than another. It is the fruit of the Spirit, *love*, which is the most important. However, there are still many who are confused on this subject, or who have been taught that all who receive the baptism of the Spirit must fit into that one pigeonhole and have the same evidence, i.e., speaking in tongues.

Let me ask you a question: Does every married couple need to carry a framed license around with them to prove that they are legally married? Doesn't the visible proof of a married couple rest in *the way they relate to one another*—even in public? That marriage license is tucked away somewhere, to be produced when needed. But if one is looking for a visible sign, it could be that *togetherness* which is based on a mutually exclusive covenant called *love*.

The classical pentecostalists (Assembly of God, Foursquare, etc.) insist that speaking in tongues is the one valid sign by which persons can know they have received the baptism of the Spirit. The neo-pentecostalists (Episcopal, Roman Catholic, Lutheran, and other denominations in the renewal movement of the past ten years) agree that most do, but some do not, and that *love for God and the brethren* is the valid sign (Romans 5:5, 1 John 3:23-24, 1 Corinthians 13:1-3). It is true that those who receive an audible gift of tongues do possess an unmistakable sign which is very real and very personal. But we could ask: a sign of what? Of having received the Holy Spirit? Of having received the baptism of the Spirit? Or of having received one of the gifts He freely gives?

Those who have not received this "sign" sometimes seek for fifteen or twenty years, believing that some sin or disobedience on their part is hindering them. This is tragic, because they are thus distorting the love and willingness of God to give this good gift to them. "If you then, who are evil, know how to give good gifts to your children, how much more will the heavenly Father give the Holy Spirit to those who ask him!" (Luke 11:13 RSV). They are also hindered from joyful discipleship because of the "cloud" hanging over them, of not having received this sign.

There is a sign which is not a gift, but a fruit.

In the ninth chapter, we discussed the difference between the gifts of the Spirit and the fruit of the Spirit. Love is the fruit of the Spirit, which is produced from the life of the vine, as Jesus explained in the fifteenth chapter of John.

Catherine Marshall in her book, *The Helper*,[1] lists five signs that indicate to a believer that he has received the Holy Spirit, and not one of them is a gift mentioned in 1 Corinthians 12 or Romans 12. Here is her list:

1. We have a new kind of love.
2. We are led by His Spirit.
3. We hear His voice.
4. We have power to witness.
5. A new help in prayer.

I like very much that Catherine Marshall listed *love*, a new kind of love, as an important sign. St. Paul does the same at the end of the chapter on all the

[1]Marshall, op. cit., p. 31.

ASK ME, LORD, I WANT TO SAY YES

gifts (1 Corinthians 12) by urging us to seek a more
excellent way, which follows immediately: the
"Love Chapter," 1 Corinthians 13.

This emphasis or priority on love for God and for
our brothers and sisters has been operative in my
own life ever since I was a teenager and received the
Holy Spirit. The *gifts* of the Spirit came at a later
date in my life.

I would like to pursue two subjects which have
been raised thus far: First, the difference between
receiving the Holy Spirit and receiving His gifts;
second, St. Paul's teaching on *love* being more
important than all the gifts.

Receiving the Holy Spirit

Jesus breathed on His disciples after His
resurrection and said, "Peace be with you. . . .
Receive the Holy Spirit" (John 20:21-22 RSV). The
rest of His message to them indicates that they
needed the Holy Spirit in order for them to fulfill
their ministry. Later, on the day of Pentecost, they
received the visible, audible evidence of the coming
of the Holy Spirit to the young church.

When do we, believers in today's church, receive
the Holy Spirit? The answer: "For by one Spirit we
were all baptized into one body—Jews or Greeks,
slaves or free—and all were made to drink of one
Spirit" (1 Corinthians 12:13 RSV). We received God's

Holy Spirit when we put our faith in Jesus Christ. For the evangelicals, this means at conversion. For the liturgical churches, this means at water baptism. The difference of opinion in this matter is one of interpretation of Scripture, and this difference serves to give us an opportunity to love one another.

Every believer who puts his faith in Jesus Christ and receives water baptism is thus baptized into the body of Christ, and receives the Father, Son, and Holy Spirit.

The problem facing us today is that many water-baptized persons (usually in infancy) who have received the Holy Spirit have never given *themselves* wholeheartedly and unreservedly to that same Holy Spirit.

This was emphasized at the Notre Dame Charismatic Conference in August, 1978, where I was asked to lead two workshops on prayer. The theme of the conference was "You Are My Witnesses." The call went out clear and loud: We have a big job to do . . . to reach the water-baptized members of the Roman Catholic church and introduce them to the resurrected Jesus, who will baptize them with His Holy Spirit and bring them to new spiritual life (Mark 1:7-8).

Here is an illustration which further clarifies the point just made. Visiting an Episcopal church in Southern California, I learned that a deaconess was in constant difficulties with the lay people she served. She herself came to me about this problem.

"How much do you love people?" I asked.

She said that she had very little, if any, to give away. I read Romans 5:5 to her:

God has poured out his love into our hearts by means of the Holy Spirit, who is God's gift to us. (Romans 5:5 TEV)

"When did you receive the Holy Spirit?" I questioned.

"When I was baptized," was her reply.

"Yes, and I suppose that was when you were an infant?"

She admitted it, and I continued, "You received the Holy Spirit then, but since that time, how much of *you* has the Holy Spirit received?"

She readily admitted that this was what she needed, to give herself, and to be indwelt by the Spirit in a consenting, cooperating way. We talked about *love* being the sign of the Spirit's presence, and about receiving the baptism of Jesus, which is the Holy Spirit. Three weeks later I received a note telling me she had attended a Roman Catholic fellowship, where she sought and received the baptism of the Spirit. A whole new love for God and for people began to flow through her!

Love is the most important of all.

Our Lord prayed for the miracle of love and unity among us in His prayer of John 17, especially verses 20-23. He taught loving one another in His discourse on the vine and the branches. "This is my commandment, that you love one another as I have loved you" (John 15:12 RSV).

John, the beloved disciple, writes that loving one another is the test of the Spirit living in us (see 1 John 3:23-24).

St. Paul taught us that we could have all the gifts of the Spirit and be lacking in *agape love* and be utterly nothing. The beloved thirteenth chapter of 1 Corinthians states that everything except love will someday be worthless. Namely, the gifts of knowledge, prophecy, understanding mysteries, having faith to remove mountains, giving away all one's possessions, speaking in tongues of men and of angels, even becoming a martyr to death. All these things gain us nothing, compared to *agape love* (the love given by the Spirit of God) which is described in the rest of that chapter.

God's kind of love
- enables us to love when we do not agree, even when we do not like one another.
- enables us to forgive from our hearts a brother who has wronged us.

- is a caring, forgiving, accepting love.
- is an attitude which flows from a heart indwelt by the Spirit of Jesus.
- cares enough to overlook and also cares enough to confront.
- does not insist that everyone must see in the Scriptures what I see.
- bears all things, believes all things.
- hopes all things, endures all things.

Love will last through time and eternity. Loving God, which means loving Jesus Christ and our brother, is the most valid sign one can possess, that the Spirit of God lives within a person.[2]

Look for love in the brother or sister who claims to be baptized by God's Holy Spirit. Let us acknowledge as brothers and sisters all who love Jesus, and welcome them into our fellowship. Our love and His will prove to the world around us that we are His children.

The paradox we face is this: Love is a free gift but that we are to exert ourselves *to live in love* is the message of the whole New Testament. Every gift and every fruit must be exercised, and used in ministry to one another, or we shall be in danger of eventually losing it. The power to exercise it, however, is imparted to us by the Holy Spirit.

How I long that my brothers and sisters in all the churches and in all the charismatic fellowships could see this truth.

[2]See Romans 5:5; 1 Corinthians 13; Galatians 5:22-23; Romans 14:17; Ephesians 5:9; 2 Timothy 1:7; John 7:38-39, 13:34-35, 17:21, 26.

God will give to all who are ready, to all who ask.

Let us no longer label people and say: Who has or who has not received the Holy Spirit?

Let us rather say: Who has given himself to Jesus?

Let us say: Who loves God and his brother?

Let us see who is following Jesus with all the "light" they now possess, and give them our patient, loving prayers.

Let us love one another, just as Christ has loved us.

Chapter Twelve

My Friends Share Their Testimonies

MRS. DANIEL S. (BETTY) CONNELLY

Betty Connelly is one of my best friends, as well as one of my prayer partners and a very gifted woman. She is the mother of three grown children; for the past three years she has been President of ECW (Episcopal Church Women) in the Southern California Episcopal Diocese. She was Presiding Officer of the 1979 Triennial Meeting of the Women of the Episcopal Church. This is the story of how God brought renewal into Betty's life and gave her a whole new ministry.

For years I was a faithful communicant and worker in the Episcopal church, enjoying God's blessing on my family and my service to the church. I helped organize women's groups, and watched educational opportunities emerge. Singing in the choir was a real joy. I loved caring for the sacred vessels and adorning the altar.

In spite of the great satisfaction I received from doing those things, there was something missing. A vacuum existed in my heart that was just not filled by a loving family and an active church life.

Only after I heard about the baptism of the Holy Spirit did I begin to understand the deep call within me. I talked with my priest who explained the Baptism to me but, perhaps because of my own biblical illiteracy, I did not seem to understand what was required of me. I only knew I wanted the reality, that new power to love God and a life filled with His Holy Spirit. I was told about the language "of the Spirit" or "tongues," so I prayed for that, but my mouth seemed to be glued shut.

About three months later, Dennis and Rita Bennett were holding a mission in a nearby parish and my husband and I went to hear them. That night, all the reading I had been doing suddenly made sense, and I knew my very own prayer language would be released. I knelt down at the back of the church all alone and prayed earnestly. My expectation was fulfilled as three non-English words came into my mind. *Yo te amo.* I was reasonably sure they were Latin, meaning, "I love thee," and decided to use them for the glory of God. For three weeks I repeated those words with praise and thanksgiving to God in my heart, and one day there it was: My tongue suddenly "tripped" and I found myself praying in an unknown or prayer language!

Later I found that *yo* (spelled "io" in Latin) meant "hurrah," and it sobered me to read on and to discover that it also indicated a cry of pain. That signified to me that *peace* is a mixture of both joy and deep sadness.

That was the beginning of my new adventure with Our Lord, one filled with joy, but also pain—the pain of growth but accompanied with a deep sense of peace. Just when I think I am doing all I can possibly do, the Lord surprises me. He says, "Yes, but not as much as I will enable you to do."

The challenge is always before me and also the promise of St. Paul, who said, "I can do all things in Him who strengthens me."

P.S. One of Betty's chief interests is speaking on the ministry of the lay person and development of gifts needed for ministry. Betty and I recently led a six-week class on this subject at our own church, St. James Episcopal, Newport Beach, which was enthusiastically received by a class of from sixty to eighty people.

Since her own experience with the Holy Spirit, God has given her the gift of "impartation" which is that of helping others receive their own gift of a prayer language.

MRS. HARRY (GRACE) McCOY

My testimony starts out like that of any typical American girl. I was born into a good family, had brothers and sisters, became a member of the Episcopal church at infant baptism, went to UCLA, joined a sorority, got married three months after graduation, and should have lived happily ever after. I had everything to make me happy: a lovely home, a loving husband, and three beautiful children.

But something was missing, and the deep dissatisfaction in my heart began to surface when I formed an attachment to the organist from whom I was taking lessons. When he left town, my whole world collapsed. What was wrong with me? I began to recognize a pattern in my life which I had not faced.

Ten years after my marriage, I had a complete mental breakdown, and the doctors said it might have been due to birth-control pills but sometimes I wonder. I was hospitalized for six weeks, given electroshock therapy, and made a fast recovery. Then I began counseling with a psychiatrist who was a warm, loving Quaker gentleman, and soon found myself dependent on him; I began to attend the Quaker church, just because I wanted to be where my doctor was. This went on for four years.

My world fell apart again when I was notified that my doctor had closed his office and moved to Canada. I went through a long period of depression, and often walked back and forth in my kitchen crying out, "What is life all about? What is the answer?"

To make a long story short, two of my friends invited me to an early Eucharist and a prayer meeting, and then to a home prayer meeting the following evening. I had been corresponding with my doctor, and that very day had received a letter from him which was very unkind and cut me off completely. I cried all day, feeling utterly alone and crushed, but I finally decided to go to that evening meeting because I had nowhere else to go and I didn't even want to live any longer.

That was the turning point in my life. They prayed for me, and laid hands on me for comfort and healing of my spirit. It was a totally new experience and I was hungry to know more. They told me about the baptism of the Holy Spirit, the living waters which Jesus promised would flow into my innermost being, and I prayed that I might receive this baptism.

Actually, it was given to me in a dream: The Lord Jesus came and laid His hands on my head, and all the sadness was gone. He filled me with His love. When I awoke, that love was still with me, and I knew I was loved unconditionally and forever.

The gift of tongues, or my prayer language, was

not given to me for several weeks. I wasn't sure I wanted it, but I left it all in the Lord's hands and was willing to receive it in His time. Then one day I felt great compassion for that doctor, and as I prayed for him, strange words began to come from my mouth and I realized the Holy Spirit was praying for that doctor through me. I had run out of my own words and ideas, and the Spirit began to give me words beyond my own understanding.

Now I experience this phenomena when I feel compassion for others and pray for them. The old tendency to attachments is sometimes there, but I know that most of all I'm attached to Jesus Christ, and I know that He is the only One that can ever give me all the love my heart desires.

Grace is one of my dear friends, my prayer partner and helper. God has given her a powerful prayer ministry and His love flows freely from her to others.

MR. AND MRS.
WALLACE R. (WALLY AND GRACE) SOLI
Wally

I grew up in a Lutheran home and did all the things I was supposed to do. I was baptized, studied the catechism, and was confirmed in the Lutheran church. As a teenager, because of close friends, I became involved in a number of youth activities at the parish hall of the neighborhood Episcopal church, and even served as an acolyte.

After Grace and I were married, and while our children were growing up, we became involved in church activities. When our children left home I seemed to hit a plateau—the things that mattered in the past and the dreams I had been chasing were no longer there. This outlook prevailed in both my home life as well as business activities. Something important was missing.

I began to stop for a drink before I went home, sometimes alone, sometimes with the fellows, in order to get the day behind me. Social events usually included cocktail parties with light chit-chat but with no depth of openly sharing real feelings. Life seemed to have lost its purpose. Drinking offered a temporary escape, but certainly offered no long-term solution. I felt I was just drifting through life with no goals or purpose. I'm sure Grace felt the same way, but I avoided any discussion regarding our relationship or future plans. Day by day we grew further apart.

After we started back to church (St. James Episcopal), I saw a nucleus of persons there who had a kind of Christianity that was real, something I wanted. I remember praying on one occasion, "Take me, Lord, my life is Yours." That seemed to open a door. I continued to attend church, always hungry for more, and never finding enough to fill that inner emptiness.

Then we both signed up for *Life in the Spirit* classes. It was at that time I really found the Holy Spirit (or He found me). At the altar when our final commitment was made, I asked Him to come in and He did. It was as if my heart were broken open, tears came, and I found myself saying over and over in Norwegian, "Jesu Novm" (Jesus' Name).

A tremendous warmth flooded me, and the next few days I walked as if on a cloud. I remember that early the following morning I found my mouth full of praise to God in a strange language that was both beautiful and satisfying. I still use it daily to give praise and thanks to Jesus.

After that, both Grace and I found further purpose and growth in our lives through making our Cursillo, attending Marriage Encounter, and Faith Alive. Our weekly sharing and praying with a loving Christian prayer group has brought a real source of strength and joy into our lives. It has only been about three years, but for us, it has been a whole new life.

Grace

I grew up in a home which was guided by good moral principles, but God and the church played no part in it. It was not until I was married and had three children that I felt the need for church attendance. Then I became involved in all the activities—church social events, ski weekends for teenagers (we lived in Washington state), helping with the youth program (weekly dinner meetings for as many as 200 young people).

During this time I was baptized and confirmed, but although church work was something I did, there was no spiritual depth in this involvement. Then we moved to California and after our youngest was confirmed our church attendance became very irregular.

The following years were busy ones; however, the inner void was growing. As the years slipped by, Wally and I seemed to be drifting apart, neither of us able to reach out and help the other: We both were hurting so much in our own individual worlds.

I remember going into Grace Cathedral in San Francisco about three years ago, at a particularly difficult time in our lives, and kneeling alone in prayer. Two organists were rehearsing for a concert and the church was filled with beautiful music. My prayer was desperate and I only said it once, "Jesus, lead me." And He did!

That was the beginning of a "new life." He began to heal us—Wally and me. We attended church together on a regular basis because we wanted to. We went to everything that was announced, for there was so much to learn and both of us had a real hunger and thirst to learn more of the Lord.

A definite period of growth came to me after the *Life in the Spirit* classes. I received the baptism of the Spirit at that time, but my prayer language (as I like to call it) was slower coming than Wally's. I finally relaxed and "let go" one day while driving down Canyon Road, and now it is available all the time. I especially use it in our prayer group when we lay hands on each other for ministry.

Conclusion

Wally is a sales manager for a national packaging company. He has been training in the Bethel Bible course for two years, and is excited about teaching a class of his own. He asks for prayer that he might be more transparent, learn to share, and be open to the guidance of the Spirit.

Grace is chairman of the Friday morning women's prayer group which meets in her home. (I am part of that group.) "I read all the good books I can, but I need to get into the Bible," Grace told me, "and I'm looking forward to being in one of the Bethel classes so I can learn more."

RECOMMENDED READING

Basham, Don, A Handbook on Holy Spirit Baptism
Published by Whitaker Books (607 Laurel Drive, Monroeville, PA 15146).
Very readable, with thirty-seven questions and answers covering every aspect of this teaching and experience.

Bennett, Dennis, Nine O'clock in the Morning
Published by Logos International, 1970. This is the best book I know for initial information.

Marshall, Catherine, The Helper
Published by Chosen Books, Inc. (Word Books, Waco, Texas), 1978. Contains most of the New Testament information on the Holy Spirit.

Sherrill, John, They Speak with Other Tongues
Published by Pillar Books (Harcourt Brace Jovanovich, Inc., New York), 1976.

The Life in the Spirit Seminars (Team Manual)
Published by Word of Life, P.O. Box 331, Ann Arbor, MI 48107. For group instruction (cassette also).

Finding New Life in the Spirit
For individuals in the above groups. Daily readings and prayers to help prepare those seeking this baptism.

For free information on how to receive
the international magazine

LOGOS JOURNAL

also Book Catalog

Write: Information

LOGOS JOURNAL CATALOG
Box 191
Plainfield, NJ 07061